First World War
and Army of Occupation
War Diary
France, Belgium and Germany

47 DIVISION
Divisional Troops
255 Machine Gun Company
12 November 1917 - 28 February 1918

WO95/2721/3

The Naval & Military Press Ltd
www.nmarchive.com
Published in association with The National Archives

Published by

The Naval & Military Press Ltd

Unit 10 Ridgewood Industrial Park,

Uckfield, East Sussex,

TN22 5QE England

Tel: +44 (0) 1825 749494

www.naval-military-press.com

www.nmarchive.com

This diary has been reprinted in facsimile from the original. Any imperfections are inevitably reproduced and the quality may fall short of modern type and cartographic standards.

© **Crown Copyright**
Images reproduced by permission of The National Archives, London, England, 2015.

Contents

Document type	Place/Title	Date From	Date To
Heading	WO95/2721/3		
Heading	47th Division 255th Machine Gun Coy. Nov 1917-Feb 1918		
War Diary	Belton Park	12/11/1917	12/11/1917
War Diary	In The Field	13/11/1917	30/11/1917
Miscellaneous	From O.C. 255th M. Guns Company	01/01/1918	01/01/1918
Heading	255th Machine Gun Company War Diary (Original) For December 1917 Vol 2		
War Diary	In The Field	01/12/1917	31/12/1917
Heading	255th Machine Gun Company War Diary For January 1918 Vol 3		
War Diary	Franvillers	01/01/1918	04/01/1918
War Diary	Line	05/01/1918	31/01/1918
Heading	War Diary Of 255th M.G. Company For February Vol 4		
War Diary	In The Field	01/02/1918	28/02/1918

WO95/2721/3

47TH DIVISION

255TH MACHINE GUN COY.

NOV 1917 - FEB 1918

47 Div
255 Machine Gun Co
Ref MGS/27

WAR DIARY or INTELLIGENCE SUMMARY.

Army Form C. 2118.

(Erase heading not required.)

Vol 1

Place	Date	Hour	Summary of Events and Information	Remarks and references to Appendices
	NOV.		NOVEMBER 1917	
BELTON PARK	12th		The Company left BELTON PARK and entrained at GRANTHAM STATION at 12.10 am. Entrainment complete in 17 minutes	
In the FIELD	13th		Arrived SOUTHAMPTON DOCK at 9.30 am. Detrained. The Company confined to the docks. Tea and dinners on the dock. Embarked on the N.W. MILLAR at 4.30 pm. Left the dock at 7 pm and laid in the SOUTHAMPTON WATER all night	
"	14th		Still in SOUTHAMPTON WATER. Rifle inspection 12 NOON. Crossed to LE HAVRE during the night	
"	15th		Disembarked at LE HAVRE at the BOOTH LINE landing stage. Disembarkation complete by 4 pm. The Company moved to No 1 Rest Camp LE HAVRE; arriving at 5.15 pm.	
"	16th		Inspection. Parade of the Company to ascertain deficiencies of kit. The adjutant went to D.A.D.O.S. and drew a quantity of kit required. The company provided 1 N.C.O. and 12 men as guard	1 O.R. Hospital
"	17th		Company parade. Fighting Order and issued with clothing and necessaries	
"	18th		Parade at 11.30 am ready to move off. O.C. Camp inspected tents. Arrived at the station 1 pm. Left at 4 pm. Stopped at BUCHY 9 pm.	

Ref m. G S/27

WAR DIARY 255 Machine Gun Coy

or INTELLIGENCE SUMMARY.

(Erase heading not required.)

Army Form C. 2118.

Instructions regarding War Diaries and Intelligence Summaries are contained in F. S. Regs., Part II. and the Staff Manual respectively. Title pages will be prepared in manuscript.

Place	Date	Hour	Summary of Events and Information	Remarks and references to Appendices
In the Field	NOV. 19th		Continued Page 2. Arrived MONT. ST. ELOI about 9 a.m. Detrained in 1½ hours. Marched to FEVRIN CAPELLE. 1, 2 and 3 Sections in huts. No 4 Section in billet. Visited by D.M.G.O. Major BOARD.	
"	20th		Cleaning up settling into billets. OC Company went to 47th Divisional HQ to see G.O.C. and Divisional staff.	
"	21st		Parades 10 a.m. and 2 p.m. Mechanism and T.A.	1. O.R. Hospital
"	22nd		Left FEVRIN CAPELLE 10.30 a.m. Marched to DAINVILLE 4.30 p.m.	
"	23rd		Inspected by G.O.C. Division 3 p.m.	1. O.R. Hospital
"	24th		Left DAINVILLE 10 a.m. marched to ACHIET LE PETIT 5.15 p.m. Billeted in huts.	
"	25th		Company proceeded on Lorries to BEAULENCOURT arriving 4.30 p.m. Billeted in huts.	
"	26th		Cleaning up in morning. Baths in afternoon for 30 men.	
"	27th		Left BEAULENCOURT at 2 p.m. marched to BEAUMETZ LES CAMBRAI.	
"	28th		BEAUMETZ LES CAMBRAI. C.O. and T.O. reconnoitred transport routes during the afternoon. Company received orders to stand by at 3.55 p.m. No 1 and 2 Sections continued.	

WAR DIARY or INTELLIGENCE SUMMARY.

255 Machine Gun Co.   Army Form C. 2118.

Place	Date	Hour	Summary of Events and Information	Remarks and references to Appendices
In the Field	Nov. 28th cont		continued page 3 and one subsection of No 3 Section moved at 7.15 p.m. relieved 10 guns of 201 M.G. Coy. in the factory on main BAPAUME CAMBRAI ROAD. Relief complete 2.10 a.m. 29th inst. Coy. HQ were at K 10 d 30.50. Rear Coy HQ heavily shelled during night at BEAUMETZ LES CAMBRAI Casualties 1. O.R. severely wounded and 2 mules killed During relief 1 O.R. No 1 Section was killed	
"	29th		Factory shelled intermittently during the day with 77 m.m. and 4.2 in. shells O.C. Company visited 6 guns about 10.30 a.m. Adjt reconnoitred routes for ration party O.C. reconnoitred new positions for guns S of the road owing to heavy shelling of the FACTORY Rear Coy. HQ moved from BEAUMETZ LES CAMBRAI to HERMIES Night of 29th-30th passed fairly quiet	
"	30th		At 5.30 a.m. O.C. No 1 Section moved his section to old GERMAN trench in E 28 b 90.15 S of CAMBRAI ROAD and thereby avoided much of the barrage At about 7.30 a.m. enemy opened intense barrage fire on Factory and surroundings and about 8 a.m. launched a series of attacks which were apparently unsuccessful. The factory and its vicinity were heavily shelled until about 12.30 p.m. C.O. and Adjt left Coy. HQ for factory about 11.0 a.m. and visited No 1 section continued	

WAR DIARY 255 Machine Gun Co.
or
INTELLIGENCE SUMMARY

Army Form C. 2118.

Place	Date	Hour	Summary of Events and Information	Remarks and references to Appendices
In the Field	Nov. 30th cont		Continued page 4 and guns in the factory. 2 guns of No 2 Section and 1 gun of No 3 Section had been knocked out. No casualties. Guns had fired 9000 rounds on barrage lines. Enemy continued intermittent shelling until dark when situation became quieter. Received orders that remaining 6 guns were to come under orders of G.O.C. 141 Bde. and move to BOURLON WOOD. Lt. DORMAN with remaining 6 guns left 141 Bde HQ at 11.0 P.M. Situation quiet during night except for intermittent shelling of valley between Company HQ and CAMBRAI ROAD. F. J. Lawrence 2nd Lt for O.C. 255 Machine Gun Co.	

From. O.C. 255th M. Gun
Company.

To. H.Q.S. 4) th
84 Division

Herewith dup.
War Diary (Original)
for December 1917.

E.C. Lewis Mgr
O.C.

WAR DIARY
or
INTELLIGENCE SUMMARY.

(Erase heading not required.)

Army Form C. 2118.

Instructions regarding War Diaries and Intelligence Summaries are contained in F. S. Regs., Part II. and the Staff Manual respectively. Title pages will be prepared in manuscript.

Vol 2

Place	Date	Hour	Summary of Events and Information	Remarks and references to Appendices
			255th. MACHINE GUN COMPANY.	
			W A R D I A R Y (ORIGINAL)	
			F O R	
			D E C E M B E R 1 9 1 7.	

WAR DIARY or INTELLIGENCE SUMMARY.

Army Form C. 2118.

(Erase heading not required.)

Place	Date 1917 Dec.	Hour	Summary of Events and Information	Remarks and references to Appendices
In the Field	1		Situation fairly quiet. D.M.G.O. & C.O. visited all guns except No.4.Section. Adjutant went to Rear H.Q., returning same day.	4 O.R. Killed. 2 O.R. Wounded. 2 O.R. Rejoined from Hospital.
	2	8-10 p.m. (Zero Hr)	Situation quiet in morning. C.O. & C.S.M. visited all guns in FACTORY & BOURLON WOOD, except those in charge of SGT. WARNER which were in advance of our front line. No.1.Section fired 1,000 rds. barrage fire on reported enemy movement. Nos.1,2, & ½-3 Sections co-operated with barrage fire in a minor operation in BOURLON WOOD & 10,000 rds. were fired.	1 O.R. Killed. 3 O.R. Wounded.
	3		Situation quiet. Adjt. & C.S.M. visited all guns in FACTORY & BOURLON WOOD except those i/c SGT.WARNER. C.O. reconnoitred new positions near ANNEUX. No.4.Section & ½-3.Section, situated in BOURLON WOOD were relieved & returned to ADVD. Coy. H.Q.	Lt. J.E.GORDON W at D.
	4		Situation still fairly quiet. C.O. visited guns in FACTORY during morning. Afternoon, orders received regarding withdrawal from the BOURLON SALIENT. C.O. reconnoitred new positions to be taken up after withdrawal, in HUGHES SWITCH by Nos. 3 & 4 Sections. Adjt. reconnoitred new ADVD Coy. H.Q. Coy. H.Q. withdrew to new position. Nos. 3 & 4 Sections proceeded to new positions in HUGHES SWITCH. Transport lines & REAR Coy. H.Q. moved to vicinity of RUYAULCOURT.	
	5	4.15 & 4.45 a.m.	No.2. Section took up anti-aircraft positions in GEORGES STREET. D.M.G.O. & C.O. reconnoitred further positions in HUGHES SWITCH. ADJT. reconnoitred positions in rear of Coy. H.Q. and also near old Coy. H.Q. No.1.Section improved & camouflaged trench around Coy. H.Q. Nos.3 & 4 Sections fired 500 rds. at enemy attempting to reconnoitre position of our new line. Nos.3 & 4 Sections fired 3,500 rds. barrage fire to cover retirement of infantry & to keep up a semblance of activity during retirement.	

WAR DIARY
or
INTELLIGENCE SUMMARY.

(Erase heading not required.)

Army Form C. 2118.

Instructions regarding War Diaries and Intelligence Summaries are contained in F. S. Regs., Part II. and the Staff Manual respectively. Title pages will be prepared in manuscript.

Place	Date DEC.17	Hour	Summary of Events and Information	Remarks and references to Appendices
In the Field	6		No.4.Section heavily shelled in HUGHES SWITCH at intervals throughout the day. C.O. visited No.2 & 4 Sections. No.2 Section started erecting island emplacements for anti-aircraft defense. No.2.Section fired 3,000 rds. harrassing fire during night behind S.O.S.lines	7.2.C.1.
"	7	6+4/am 1pm.	HUGHES SWITCH heavily shelled between C.O. visited all Sections. No.2.Section relieved No.4.Section in HUGHES SWITCH. C.O. & Adjt., went up to HUGHES SWITCH, & found No.2.Section had been heavily shelled while relieving, causing a certain amount of confusion.	71.C.1. 4 O.R.Wounded.
"	8	7.30pm	HUGHES SWITCH again shelled at intervals by 77 & 105 mm. guns. C.O. visited No.1 & 3 Sections. Adjt visited No.4.Section. S.O.S. answered by 1 & 3 Sections with 5,000 rds.	1 O.R. Killed. 1 O.R. Wounded. 7.2.C.1.
"	9	8.am	Night quiet. Hostile Attack under cover of heavy artillery barrage on outpost in front of HUGHES SWITCH, guns fired 4,500 rds. on S.O.S.lines. C.O. visited guns in HUGHES SWITCH during attack. Remainder of day fairly quiet except for intermittent shelling.	1 O.R. Killed 1 O.R. Wounded. P.3.C.1.
"	10		Intermittent shelling during morning. C.O. visited 1 & 2 Sections. Adjt. visited No.4. Section. No.3.Section relieved No.2 Section in HUGHES SWITCH.	2/Lt Dowson. reptd, for duty from M.G.Base 4 O.R Wounded. 1 O.R. A/Wounded. LT.W.R.L. HUTCHINGS W. at D
"	11.	3.10pm	Situation normal. C.O. visited 1 & 3 Sections. Adjt. visited 2 & 4 Sections Nos.1 & 3 Sections with drawn at dusk from HUGHES SWITCH. All guns answered S.O.S. Signal with 5,000 rds. No hostile action developed.	Lt.W.S.SMITH. reptd for duty from, M.G. Base. 1 O.R. Wounded.
"	12.		Night fairly quiet. C.O. visited all Sections & reconnoitered new positions for No.3 Section behind HINDENBURG SUPPORT. No.1. Section relieved by 4 guns of No.6.Coy. & proceeded at dusk to WAGON lines. No.3.Section moved to new position reconnoitered by C.O. as above.	3 O.R. To Hospital. 1 O.R. Wounded.

WAR DIARY
or
INTELLIGENCE SUMMARY.

(Erase heading not required.)

Army Form C. 2118.

Instructions regarding War Diaries and Intelligence Summaries are contained in F. S. Regs., Part II. and the Staff Manual respectively. Title pages will be prepared in manuscript.

Place	Date DEC. 17.	Hour	Summary of Events and Information	Remarks and references to Appendices
In the Field	13	8.30 a.m.	Artillery "Crash" on hostile line in front of GRAINCOURT. C.O. visited No.3.Section, in new position. Adjt. visited Nos.2 & 4 Sections. Anti-aircraft positions & trenches in their vicinity improved & Camouflaged.	P.3.C.L. 4 O.R. To Hospital.
	14		Situation quiet. 2 & 4 Sections fired 7,000 rds. harassing fire on area behind S.O.S. lines during night of 13-14th. C.O. visited all Sections. No.3. Section improved & camouflaged emplacements.	1 O.R. Rejoined from Hospital. P.3.C.L.
	15		Intermittent hostile shelling. Hostile aircraft active in early morning. Nos. 2 & 4 Sections fired 10,000 rds harassing fire during night of 14 - 15th. on area behind S.O.S. lines. C.O. visited all Sections. Nos. 2 & 4 Sections heavily shelled for 3 hrs. during the forenoon with 5.9cm.	P.3.C.L.
	16	8.30 p.m.	Situation quiet. C.O. visited No.3.Section. Adjt visited Nos.2 & 4 Sections. No.3.Section relieved by a section of 140 Coy. Nos.2 & 4 Sections relieved by one section of 141 Coy. Relief complete. H.Q., Nos.2,3, & 4 Sections marched independently to wagon lines.	1. O.R. To Hospital. P.3.C.L.
	17		Snow fell heavily during night. Coy. proceeded by motor lorry from wagon lines to BRUCE HUTS in BOUZINCOURT AREA. Transport proceeded to same place by March Route. G.O.C. Divn. inspected huts.	P.3.C.L.
	18		All Sections employed on cleaning up & checking gun kit & improving condition of huts and surroundings.	P.3.C.L.
	19	10-12.30 p.m. 2-2.45 p.m.	Section Parades. Checking Gun Kit, Cleaning up and pay.	P.3.C.L.
	20	10-12.30 p.m. 2-2.45 p.m.	Section Parades. Infantry Drill, Gun Drill, and Cleaning Guns.	1. O.R. To Hospital. P.3.C.L.
	21	10-12.30 p.m. 2-2.45 p.m.	Section Parades. I.A., Mechanism, and Lecture.	P.3.C.L.

WAR DIARY or INTELLIGENCE SUMMARY.

(Erase heading not required.)

Army Form C. 2118.

Instructions regarding War Diaries and Intelligence Summaries are contained in F. S. Regs., Part II. and the Staff Manual respectively. Title pages will be prepared in manuscript.

Place	Date Dec. 17	Hour	Summary of Events and Information	Remarks and references to Appendices
In the Field	22		Coy. moved by march route to billets at FRANVILLERS. Transport moved separately owing to extreme slipperiness of roads.	P.3.C.L.
"	23		Settling into Billets. Arranging Xmas festivities. Divine Service.- C. of E. parade in Salle de Bal, FRANVILLERS. R.C. parade at Parish Church.	1 O.R. To Hospital. P.3.C.L.
"	24	9.45 - 12.30 p.m. 2 - 2.45 p.m.	Section Parades. Inspections, Drill? Cleaning up & Mechanism.	2 O.R. To Hospital. P.3.C.L.
"	25	10.0 a.m. 1.0 p.m.	Xmas Day. Troops in good spirits. G.O.C. visited unit, to give Xmas Greetings. Divine Service.- C. of E. parade & Holy Communion in Salle de Bal, FRANVILLERS. R.C. parade in the Parish Church. Special Xmas Dinner for troops. C.O. ~~visited~~ & Adjt., visited all men during dinners.	1 O.R. To Hospital. P.3.C.L.
"	26	9.30 - 12.30 p.m. 2 - 2.45 p.m.	Section Parades.- Inspections, Gun Drill? I.A., Mechanism & Belt Filling.	3 O.R. To Hospital. P.3.C.L.
"	27	9.30 - 12.30 p.m. 2 - 2.45 p.m.	Section Parades.- Inspections, I.A., Gun Drill, Mechanism & Handling of Arms. Barns, Cookhouses & Latrines whitewashed. C.O. attended Divnl Conference & Tactical Ex.	1 O.R. To Hospital. P.3.C.L.
"	28	9.30 - 12.30 p.m. 2 - 2.45 p.m.	Section Parades.- Inspections, Mechanism, I.A., & Lecture on Characteristics of M.Gun, Company Drill.	1 O.R. To Hospital. P.3.C.L.
"	29	9.30 - 12.30 p.m.	Section Parades.- Inspections, Belt Filling, Washing & Creasing Limbers.	P.C.L. 1 O.R. Rejoined from Hospital.
"	30		Divine Services) C. of E. parade in Salle de Bal, FRANVILLERS. R.C. parade in Parish Church.	1 O.R. To Hospital. P.3.C.L.
"	31	9.30 - 12.30 p.m. 2 - 2.45 p.m. 6.30 p.m.	Section Parades.- Inspections, Gun Drill, Stripping, Mechanism, & Handling of Arms. No.3.Section bathed. Coy. Concert in the Salle de Bal.	1 O.R. To Hospital. P.3.C.L.

1.1.18.

P.E.C. Lewis Major.
O.C.

ORIGINAL

255th Machine Gun Company Vol 3

War Diary

for

January 1918

Divisional H.Q.

WAR DIARY or INTELLIGENCE SUMMARY.

Army Form C. 2118.

Instructions regarding War Diaries and Intelligence Summaries are contained in F. S. Regs., Part II. and the Staff Manual respectively. Title pages will be prepared in manuscript.

(Erase heading not required.)

Place	Date	Hour	Summary of Events and Information	Remarks and references to Appendices
FRANVILLERS	Jan 1st	-	Company on the Range during the morning. Afternoon Care and Cleaning.	P.C.
	2nd	-	Section Parades. 9.30-12.30p; 2-2.45 pm. Belt filling Section Drill. I.A. Mechanism. N°3 Section Baths	P.C.
	3rd	-	Morning Range. N°1 Section Baths. Afternoon Care and Cleaning.	P.C.
	4th	-	The Coy. left Billets at 11.15 am. entrained at MERICOURT L'ABBÉ; detrained at YTRES 9.30 pm. Marched to BERTINCOURT. Sgt WARNER and Pte SUTTON awarded MILITARY MEDAL.	P.C. 2 O.R. Hospital
line	5th	-	N°S. 1, 2. and 4 Sections proceeded to the FLESQUERIERES -RIBÉCOURT LINE. relieving the 57th M.G.Coy	P.C.
	6th	-	FLESQUIERES intermittently shelled also RIBÉCOURT.	P.C.
	7th	-	C.O. left for Division to take over duties of A/D.M.G.O.	P.C. 1 O.R. Hospital
	8th	-	Day quiet. Heavy snowfall and blizzard.	P.C.

WAR DIARY or INTELLIGENCE SUMMARY.

Army Form C. 2118.

(Erase heading not required.)

Place	Date	Hour	Summary of Events and Information	Remarks and references to Appendices
Line	9th	—	Barrage positions reconnoitred. Readjustment of M.Gun positions.	P/Ch
	10th	—	No 3 Section worked on Barrage positions. All guns withdrawn from forward positions by 5 pm. No 1 Section to Wagon lines. No 4 Section remain as working party. No 2 Section took over New E Battery position. No 3 Section D. Battery position. RIBÉCOURT shelled.	1 O.R. Wounded. P/Ch.
	11th	—	D and E Batteries laid on S.O.S. lines by 8 am No 4 Section returned to the wagon lines at dusk. Adjt visited all positions.	4 O.R Hospital P/Ch
	12th	—	Adjt visited all gun positions. RIBÉCOURT was shelled. Batteries connected by telephone to Battalions and Company H.Qrs.	P/Ch 2. O.R. Hospital

WAR DIARY
or
INTELLIGENCE SUMMARY.

Army Form C. 2118.

(Erase heading not required.)

Place	Date	Hour	Summary of Events and Information	Remarks and references to Appendices
Line	13th		UNSEEN TRENCH shelled with 5.9" shells.	PCh.
	14th		Gun positions visited by O.C. D. and E Batteries registered at 4 pm. Results satisfactory. Nos 1 and 4 Sections came from Wagon Lines and were amalgamated into one Section.	5. OR. Reinforcements PCh 10.R. Reinforcement.
	15th		No 2 Section relieved by Composite Section at 7.30 pm.	PCh.
	16th		H.Qrs. D. Battery moved to RAVINE AVENUE. Gas shells fell near RAVINE AVENUE about 4 pm.	PCh. PCh.
	17th		Coy H.Q. move to catacombs at RIBÉ COURT. D. Battery shelled for five minutes at 4 pm.	PCh.
	18th		Clearance of D. Battery over E Battery tested with satisfactory results.	PCh.

WAR DIARY or INTELLIGENCE SUMMARY.

Army Form C. 2118.

Place	Date	Hour	Summary of Events and Information	Remarks and references to Appendices
Line	19th		"D" Battery shelled between 4 pm and 5 pm. G.O.C. visited Advanced Coy H-Qrs. in the morning	5.O.R. Reinforcements 1.O.R. from Hospital P/Ch.
	20th		No 2 Section relieve No 3 Section at "D" Battery	P/Ch.
	21st		Quiet day.	P/Ch. 1.O.R. Wd.
	22nd		H.Qrs. baths. and clean clothing. Situation quiet throughout the day.	1.O.R. leave. 1.O.R. Wd. at duty P/Ch. 1.O.R. to Hospital.
	23rd		O.C. visited guns. Hostile Artillery active in vicinity of Batteries	P/Ch.
	24th		Situation very quiet.	P/Ch.
	25th		Composite Section relieved by No 3 Section. TRESCAULT bombed by E.A.	P/Ch.
	26th		Misty day visibility bad.	P/Ch. 4.O.R. from Base

WAR DIARY
or
INTELLIGENCE SUMMARY.

(Erase heading not required.)

Army Form C. 2118.

Instructions regarding War Diaries and Intelligence Summaries are contained in F. S. Regs., Part II. and the Staff Manual respectively. Title pages will be prepared in manuscript.

Place	Date	Hour	Summary of Events and Information	Remarks and references to Appendices
Line	27th		Hostile Artillery quiet. "D" and "E" Batteries carried out harrassing fire in conjunction with Artillery Dvsgt.	B.C.
	28th		C.O and D.M. C.O visited batteries during morning.	P.C.
	29th		C.O. visited batteries. Situation quiet.	P.C.
	30th		Coy H.Q. shelled about 7 pm with gas shells. Nos. 1 and 4 Sections relieved Nos 2 and 3 Sections. Relief complete 8.35pm	P.C. 1.O.R. Hospital
	31st		Coy H.Q. moved to L.25.a.76.76. Batteries carried out harrassing fire at night.	P.C.

2.2.18.

P.B.C. Lewis Major
Cmdg 255th Army Bde Coy.

ORIGINAL

Confidential.

WAR DIARY

OF

255th M.G. Company.

FOR

FEBRUARY.

WAR DIARY or INTELLIGENCE SUMMARY.

Army Form C. 2118.

No. 255 MACHINE GUN COY. MACHINE GUN CORPS

Place	Date	Hour	Summary of Events and Information	Remarks and references to Appendices
In the Field	1918 Feby 1		O.C. visited O.P. and Batteries. "D" Battery was shelled in the early morning with GAS shells	1 O.R. to 1st A. 6 O.R. from Base Embarkment 2 O.R to Hosp. 2 Lt Downer to Hospital
do.	2nd		Batteries visited by O.C. FLESQUIERES and RIBECOURT shelled intermittently throughout morning	
do.	3rd		O.C. made tour of Guns. D & E Batteries fired harrassing on ORIVAL WOOD during night	1 O.R to Hospital
do.	4th	about 5 am	Batteries visited by C.O. "D" Battery shelled with Gas shells about 5 am. about 30 shells fell	
do.	5th	about 4 pm	The O.C. made a tour of the trenches in the morning. The D.M.G.O. visited advanced posts during day. Nos 2 & 3 Sections relieved D & E Batteries respectively in the evening. 2/Lt Smith reconnoitred "E" Batteries position during afternoon for O.C. No 3 Section. A good number of gas shells fell between the Brasseries and Havrincourt Road about 4 pm.	
do.	6th	1-0 am	Both batteries visited by O.C. during morning. "E" Battery carried out harrassing fire programme at night firing 3500 rounds. The S.O.S. was also answered by "E" Battery 3000 rounds being fired at 1-0 am. "D" Battery also carried out harrassing fire programme 2750 rounds being expended.	1 O.R. Wounded Remaining on duty.

WAR DIARY
or
INTELLIGENCE SUMMARY.

(Erase heading not required.)

Army Form C. 2118.

No. 255 MACHINE GUN COY.
MACHINE GUN CORPS

Instructions regarding War Diaries and Intelligence Summaries are contained in F. S. Regs., Part II. and the Staff Manual respectively. Title pages will be prepared in manuscript.

Place	Date	Hour	Summary of Events and Information	Remarks and references to Appendices
In the Field	Feby 7th.	about 8-10 pm	O.C. made a tour of the Batteries in the morning "D" Battery shelled briskly about 8-10 p.m. S.O.S answered by "D" Battery in 4 Secs. R.E's ceased work on No.1 concrete emplacement	1 O.R. to Hosp. War Hospital Denisburg
do.	8th.		O.C. visited gun positions during morning. D.M.G.O. visited Coy. H.Q.	11 O.R to Hospital
do.	9th.		O.C. visited Batteries	1 O.R. to Hospital
do.	10th.		O.C. made tour of Batteries. Harrassing fire programme carried out about 2-500 rounds per Battery fired. This was carried in conjunction with artillery. "D" Battery heavily shelled about mid-day. C.H.Q also received attention from Hostile Artillery. C.O. relieved by Captain Sharp.	2 O.R. to Hosp. 9 O.R. Reinforcements
do.	11th.	about 9 pm	Both Batteries visited by C.O. During day Nos 1 & 4 Sections Relieved E & D Batteries respectively during the evening. About 40 GAS shells fell in area South of D position about 9-0 pm. E Battery Situation Normal.	
do.	12th.		O.C. visited all the gun Positions during the morning. Situation normal.	
do.	13th.		O.C. visited all the Gun Positions during the morning. Situation normal. Captain Sharp to depot relieved by Captain Gordon.	
do.	14th		C.O. visited both Batteries in the morning. Divisional Commander visited E Battery. A few shells fell near E Battery during the night.	2 Dr. R'ments

WAR DIARY or INTELLIGENCE SUMMARY.

(Erase heading not required.)

Army Form C. 2118.

Place	Date	Hour	Summary of Events and Information	Remarks and references to Appendices
In The Field	Feby. 15th		C.O. visited both Batteries. Hostile artillery considerably more active on usual targets throughout the day. Hostile aeroplanes also active.	1 O.R. to Hospital
do.	16th		C.O. visited both Batteries during morning. Hostile artillery and aircraft again active on forward and back areas.	4 O.R. to Hosp. 2/Lt. O.P. Smith to Hospital
do.	17th		C.O. visited both batteries. Nos 3 & 2 Sections relieved Nos 1 & 4 Sections in E. & D. Battery positions on night of 17-18. Hostile artillery less active during the day.	
do.	18th	about 7pm	Day fairly quiet except for some heavy shelling of R.18½ COURT in the afternoon. C.O. visited both batteries during the morning. Hostile aeroplanes passed over our lines about 7 p.m.	Lt. & P. Hutchings 1 O.R. Wounded
do.	19th	about 9-30 am	C.O. visited both batteries during morning. TANK "ENERGETIC" blown up by P.E's in at 9-30 am. Batteries carried out harrassing fire at night on round in I.14.a. & I.8.d. Some hostile M.G. bullets fell round D. battery during the night.	Lt. Hutchings to Hospital 1 O.R. to Hosp. 1 O.R. Rejoined
do.	20th		Day quiet. C.O. visited both Batteries during day. D.M.G.O. & D.M.G.O. 63rd Naval Division visited H.Q's. Night quiet.	1 O.R. to Hosp. 1 O.R. Rejoined 1 O.R. Wounded

WAR DIARY or INTELLIGENCE SUMMARY.

Army Form C. 2118.

(Erase heading not required.)

Place	Date	Hour	Summary of Events and Information	Remarks and references to Appendices
In the field	Feb 21st		Shelling brisk during morning on FLESQUIERES and just forward of E Battery. D.M.G.O. and Divisional M.G. Battalion Commander visited H.Q's. 2/Lt FITZGERALD 188th Coy 63rd Division visited H.Q's to arrange relief. C.O. visited Batteries.	1 O.R. Rejoined
do.	22nd		Hostile Shelling practically NIL. C.O. 188th M.G. Coy visited H.Q's to make further arrangements regarding relief. C.O. visited both Batteries. D. & E. Batteries relieved by 6 guns 188th M.G. Coy. Relief Complete. Nos 3 & 2 Sections and H.Q's proceeded by march route to WAGON LINES.	1 O.R. Accidentally Wounded
do.	23rd		Company moved by march Route at rear of 14th Inf. Brigade from RUYAULCOURT to KNIGHTSBRIDGE Barracks, ROCQUIGNY via YTRES - BUS and Rocquigny. Camp reached at 5.30 p.m. Four companies of Division all in camp together to form M.G. Battalion under command of Lt. Col. W.J.N. DAVIS D.S.O. The Connaught Rangers. MAJOR A.E.C. LEWIS appointed 2nd I/C Battalion. LT. C.J. FREEMAN appointed T.O. Captain E.R.A. GORDON to command Company. LT R.L. BROWN to be 2nd I/C. 1 Field Cooker attached for duty to Company.	1 O.R. to Hospital
do.	24th		Section Parades 9 - 12.30, 2 - 3. Church Parades and Cleaning of Gun Kit and Equipment	3 O.R. to Hospital

WAR DIARY or INTELLIGENCE SUMMARY.

(Erase heading not required.)

Army Form C. 2118.

Place	Date	Hour	Summary of Events and Information	Remarks and references to Appendices
In the Field	Feby 25th		Section Parades. 9 am 7-3-30. 3-30. Washing and greasing limbers and straightening of wagon lines. Inspections of Kit and Gun Equipments.	
do	26th		Section Parades 9 am 10 am 2-30 pm. Completion of washing and greasing limbers. Examining and refilling belts. Company inspection in fighting order.	
do	27th		Section Parades 8-45 am 9 am 10 am 11 am 2 pm. General Section Inspections, Gun Drill I.a. Fire orders and Company Inspection in fighting order.	
do	28th		Section Parades 8-45 am 9 am 10 am 11 am 12 noon 1-30 pm 2 pm. General Section Inspections. Physical training. Cleaning belts. Lecture "Iron hand in tight." Gas Drill and Baths for 2 & 3 Sections. Nos 1 & 4 Sections parade for Squad Drill.	

E. M. Lyndon Capt.
O.C.
No. 255 Machine Gun Coy.

www.ingramcontent.com/pod-product-compliance
Lightning Source LLC
Chambersburg PA
CBHW081250170426
43191CB00037B/2111